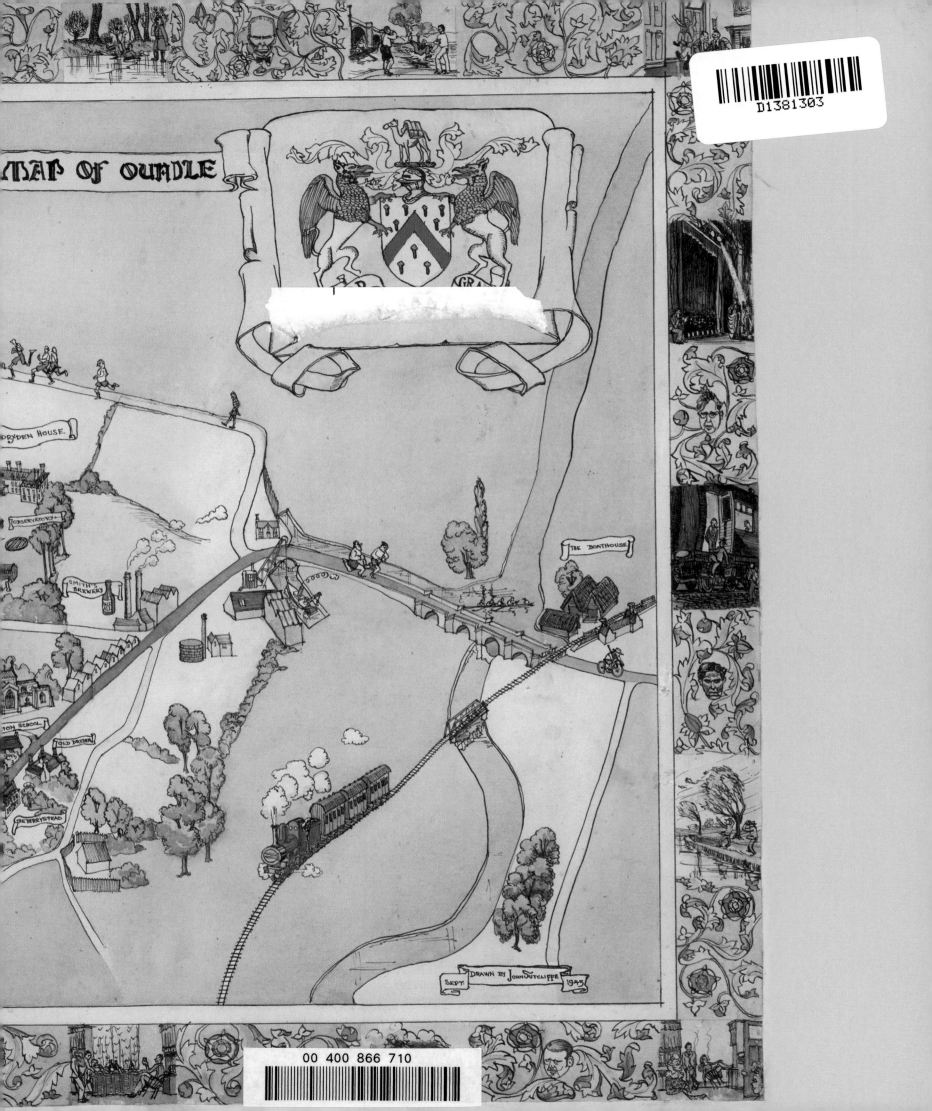

MAP OF OUNDLE

DRYDEN HOUSE.

OBSERVATORY

SMITH'S BREWERY

THE BOATHOUSE

...TON SCHOOL

OLD DRYDEN

THE BERRYSTEAD

SEPT. DRAWN BY JOHN SUTCLIFFE 1943

oundle

A SCHOOL FOR ALL SEASONS

oundle

A SCHOOL FOR ALL SEASONS

Edited by Stephen Forge

Photography by Julian Andrews

III THIRD MILLENNIUM
PUBLISHING, LONDON

Oundle
A School for all Seasons

Copyright © Oundle School and
Third Millennium Publishing Ltd

First published in 2005 by Third Millennium Publishing Ltd,
a subsidiary of Third Millennium Information Ltd

2–5 Benjamin Street
London
EC1M 5QL
www.tmiltd.com

ISBN: 1 903942 37 3

Designed and produced by Third Millennium Publishing
Printed and bound by MKT PRINT d.d., Slovenia

Endpapers: Map of Oundle (1945), by John Sutcliffe
(St Anthony, '41)

contents

foreword
Lord Renton

Although it is now more than seventy years since I faced the challenge of my first days at Oundle and that of fitting into the School House routine of the 1920s, my own impressions of my years in the School remain as indelibly vivid as those given by the photographs by Julian Andrews which follow. I am certain that although many people have passed, and things have disappeared or changed beyond recognition since those times, there will be constants relating to the changing seasons and their Oundle associations which will strike a chord with all those who have been fortunate enough to share the experience of an Oundle education.

I commend this volume and its kaleidoscope of faces past and present to all, whether they are familiar with the School or not, as an appealing reflection of the life of an institution to which I and many others owe a great deal. As a visual homage to its customs, traditions, staff and, of course, its boys and girls who will carry with them its legacy into the future, it is a fascinating gallery.

The Rt Hon. David Renton KBE QC, School House '27
The House of Lords, June 2005

editor's preface
Stephen Forge

Our purpose in the production of this book has been to present an affectionate and informal image of a year at Oundle School, reflecting not only the seasons and their landmarks but also the progress of the pupils through the system, from tentative arrivals to more confident departures. Reminiscences from Old Oundelians of several generations reinforce impressions both of the changes the School has undergone over the last 75 years and of the immutables. As the School moves into yet another era with the development of SciTec, this has been an opportunity to appreciate how that project is part of a natural progression from the educational theory of Frederick Sanderson at the turn of the twentieth century to the scientific challenges of a new millennium. Throughout the production of this book the keenness of former pupils to record their memories of the School has been overwhelming, and we hope that the sparklingly dynamic photographs of Julian Andrews will serve to fix those of the current generation of pupils.

Stephen Forge,
Oundle School Archives
July 2005

autumn

DIARY ENTRY 23 September 1942: 'FIRST day at
Oundle. Got up at 7.45am. In MORNING, Got CAP
At Moore's IN MARKET PLACE, had service in Great
Hall, and then Mr. SAUNDERS and Dr Fisher
addressed new boys. Got wet returning. In aft,
learnt rugby football. Had tea in house near
St Anthony's House. Had no prep but I had
to ring bell and am tidy boy this week.
Went up to bed 8.45 pm. Antanarivo captured.'
(Derek Way, Sidney, '47)

I arrived by the school train at the start of my first term. I had never been to Oundle. I was just 5ft. Not knowing where Grafton was, I asked the way. 'Don't speak to me, tick, unless I speak to you' was the reply!

Robert Robertson, Grafton '56

I arrived at Oundle for my first term by train in September 1947. It was dark, several hundred boys started to walk from the station up to the town. 'Do you know where School House is?' I asked a boy nearby. 'Follow me,' he said. It later transpired he didn't know either.

Paul Rooksby, School House '51

*It was compulsory to have a cold bath every morning in Crosby.
These were hip-baths (there was only one full-length 'proper' bath in
the house). However, all one mostly did was dip a few inches of one's
posterior in the bath, so it was not as arduous as it now sounds.*

Archie Burdon-Cooper, Crosby '55

*I was the first new boy – joining the Berrystead with 'Gosher' Brown
– not to wear an Eton collar. 'Bud' Fisher thought I was too tall!*

Bob Bradbury, School House '37

Two specific initiations in our first weeks in Sanderson in 1943 were 'gridding' and 'draining'. Both were washroom sports. 'Draining' entailed being laid head upstream in the large open gulley that took the water from the sports changing-room footbaths. While your head was held down by somebody's heel all the baths were emptied in one big whoosh and you were stuck under the flood. 'Gridding' was a slower torture. You were laid in an ordinary bath and the wooden foot grid was placed across the top and firmly held down. Then, forgetting the wartime 'five inch' rule, the bath was filled to the very brim with you slowly being immersed beneath. You could scream your protests through the gaps in the wood, but that only invited a glass of water in the face.

Maurice Dybeck, Sanderson '48

PREFECT (returned to Dormitory) : WHY HAS NOBODY HAD A COLD BATH?

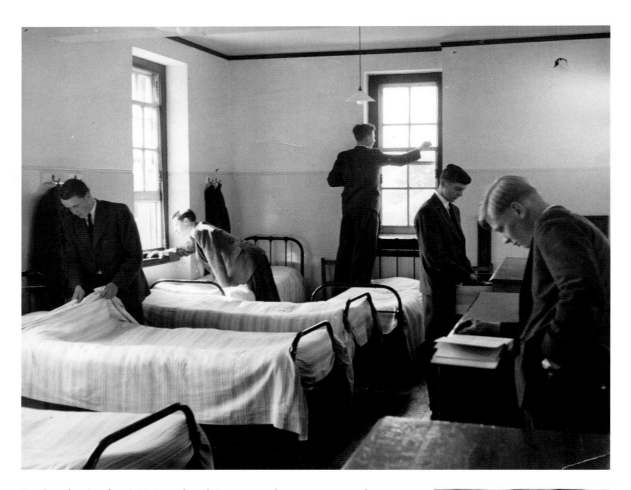

In Crosby in the 1950s, plumbing was elementary, and hip-baths, filled with cold water the night before, were obligatory for all each morning. The fifteen most junior inmates had to be up and dressed, to call out the time until breakfast at strict one-minute intervals, so that their seniors could judge their arrival to a nicety.

Barry Stobart-Hook, Crosby '58

"AHMAN, THERE'S TOO MUCH WATER BEING USED."
[WE SHALL SOON HAVE TO RESORT TO THIS.]

Sanderson House
Oundle
~~and the~~ School
~~Oundle~~
Northants

21/9/47

Dear Mum & Dad

I have settled down alright.
There are five new boys in Sanderson and I am
the senior one. I am in form Cvb, which is
about six above the bottom one. There are
several customs which are new boys are not allowed
to have their hands in their pockets and you have
to have all your buttons done up, and you have
to learn all the boys names within four weeks. I am
in the choir as a treble and we are singing the Messiah
this term.

John Robinson, Sanderson '52

'Cuts' Cutcliffe was my Mr Chips and my Cape Canaveral and may the Lord forgive me that I never told him so. But then Oundle was shot through with such wonderful people.

Christopher Campbell Thomson, Grafton '50 on behalf of
David Thomson, Sidney '18 (deceased) and
Francis Thomson, Grafton '52 (deceased)

'Cabby' Marshall taught French using a system he called his Essentials, the learning of which, he said, would stop us making the typical Englishman's mistakes when trying to speak French. The only one that comes to mind now is not to say or write 'Please lay another egg' instead of 'Please reply' by confusing répondre and repondre. When, for our set book, we started to study Prosper Mérimée's 'Colomba', 'Cabby' provided a silent action sideshow to illustrate the words we were reading in our stumbling French, like a drunken version of those solemn people who today provide sign language interpretations of boring political speeches. However, as soon as Columba herself was, so to speak, on stage, 'Cabby' moved from dumb show into full throttle acting, punctuating his heroine's adventures amongst the Corsican bandits with great girlish sighs and piercing shrieks.

David McFetrich, Bramston '56

As soon as I arrived at Oundle School in 1945, aged thirteen, I was stood on the prep room desk and made to make my first speech surrounded by a horde of jeering schoolboys. Quite terrifying!

Michael Laurens, St Anthony '50

On Sunday afternoons we junior boys would sit together in the Preproom, salivating, waiting, hoping to hear our names bellowed through the corridors as we savoured the smell of sausages and bacon wafting from the senior boys' studies. A Sunday afternoon call was invariably to collect a delicious fried reward for having given good fagging service during the previous week.

Philip Bambury, School House '61

Fagging and bell-boy duties in arctic conditions – what memories! Cooking over temperamental primuses; scouring basins, cleaning boots, sweeping changing-rooms; struggling to ring the ship's bell which regulated house activities – all to the awesome standards imposed by the prefects.

Richard Rumary, Laundimer '59

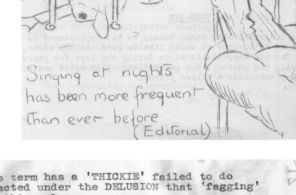

Singing at nights has been more frequent than ever before (Editorial)

Not for the first time this term has a 'THICKIE' failed to do what he has been told and acted under the DELUSION that 'fagging' takes precedence over everything else.
    This is NOT the fault of the prefects ,who arefully aware that, if they insist on fagging taking precedence,it will be stopped entirely

    Fags are warned that if this occurs again they will be dealt with by me for deliberate disobedience.

    Remember   Bank,clean clothes,attention in medicine room and anything of this nature comes FIRST.

I became a dab hand at making scrambled egg from USA dried egg, which was occasionally available in the 'Bundles for Britain' parcels from the States. This earned me a larger end-of-term tip from the prefect for whom I fagged.

Gordon Brooker, Laundimer '44

The Tuck Shop was a haven. The beans on fried bread for sixpence and the marmalade, butter and two rolls for twopence were something to dream about.

Richard Myott, School House '48

I was in Crosby 1966 to 1971, and in my last year rowed in the 1st VIII. One of my abiding memories was going into the Tuck Shop, directly after training at Tansor, with the rest of the crew, and ordering pints of milk which we would down in one. This spectacle always seemed to attract envious glances (being a 1st team, we were allowed into the Tuck Shop still in our kit, without having to change first), and was no doubt our way of displaying our macho credentials.

John Granger, Crosby '71

My first errand as a fag in 1936 was to go and buy a 'hafdee bun' from the Tuck Shop. On purchasing one and asking the price I was rewarded with a look of surprise and amusement. School slang for a penny was a 'dee' (d) and 1/2d (ha'penny) was of course a hafdee.

Anthony Butcher, St Anthony '39

Apart from some fruit I withdrew and I packet of Mark's and Spencers peanuts (I swopped for some orange) I am desperatly running short of Tuck. Please send some Tuck and something to drink. The masters are very pleasant here

Charles Higham, New House '77

I recall the day in School House when we all had starched napkins at lunch, as King Peter of Yugoslavia was calling to visit his two younger brothers, and the juniors took it in turn to paddle the ice and salt machine for the top table's ice cream.

Richard Myott, School House '48

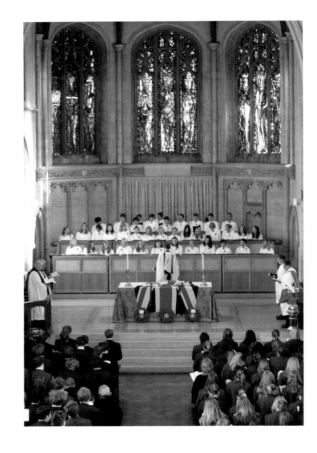

Inter-house rugger matches were important. Teams would make their way from their houses to the pitch through the streets of the town in proud, determined, fifteen-boys-wide phalanxes, ready to sweep aside all comers, not least their prospective opponents.

Philip Bambury, School House '61

winter

'Winter 1936/7. New House dormitories in Cottesmore, early MORNING. 'Healthy' open windows. Prestigious to be last to get up. Disparaging cries of "Streak...Streak" for early risers. Get up, compulsory dip in ice-cold water. Dry, dress, including stiff collar and tie (stud&co.). Dash across to main house for breakfast. Just possible minimum time, 4 minutes 30 seconds.'

(Ronald Grant, New House '38)

An unusual and prolonged cold spell of winter floods in the Lent Term of 1940 resulted in skating on the fields and Biggin Lake. The Headmaster (Bud Fisher) was keen on skating and decreed that every afternoon would be given to that activity with lessons being taken late afternoon. The snow on the roads was so compacted that some masters skated or went on skis to classes.

John Shaw, Crosby '44

Bitterly cold, the River Nene in flood, full of ice floes. Bramston, captain P.M.O. Massey, pulled ahead, we caught up. George Huse, Laxton coach, and Dudley Heesom, Bramston housemaster, frantic on the bank. DEAD HEAT! Didn't we enjoy those hot hip-baths!

John Godwin, Laxton '47

One of the greater adventures was the freeze-up in about 1962. We skated for nearly six weeks on the gravel pits, and even held a house ice-hockey competition. Unfortunately, the weather beat us to the final and that game was never played.

Peter Leach, St Anthony '63

I managed to get some skating on Sunday on very thin ice about 1¾". It was creaking & crack the whole time but the layer of snow on top rather spoilt the surface. At the moment there is no snow here whatever and there has only been a very little since I came back. I also managed to get a little skating this afternoon on a small flood there was a wonderful surfaced but not enough of it.

John Robinson, Sanderson '52

Wednesday afternoon and Friday morning CCF parades always began with the sound of iron shod (and highly polished) boots stamping and sliding on the stone floors of the house corridor.

Barry Stobart-Hook, Crosby '58

On that Parade Ground I was a Zulu. And I've loathed cocoa ever since. M.C. thought we should re-enact Rorke's Drift for a tattoo. I had a cardboard spear (Workshops Mark 1, Zulus for the equipping of) and I leapt into the searchlights like Chaka himself. At one time we threatened to overturn history by winning, but dutifully fell back when we saw an apoplectic M.C. hurling imprecations at the stockade.

Roger Freebairn, Crosby '55

Marching during O.T.C. Field Days (that dates me!) commanded by
Mr 'Snip-snap' Priestman who had a slight lisp. Kept in step by chanting
'thnip-thnip-thnip thnap thnip', which infuriated him! Belated apologies!

Lt Cdr Ken MacKenzie, Sanderson '42

Field day was always a bit of a farce, but never criticised for it meant a day off lessons. One minute, we would be hurtling down a lane in a personnel carrier and the next crawling through some particularly damp undergrowth, without really knowing what it was all about.

Christopher Pain, Sanderson '52

At Oundle we were encouraged to work at hobbies and so I was busy building radio sets. I was allowed to keep a spare room in the boarding house for my radio. During the General Strike of 1926 when there were no newspapers, the Housemaster, his assistant and any other masters around had to come to my radio room to hear the news.

George Hodson, Bramston '27

For a couple of years, I was the individual that was responsible for the music that was played before each of the school films that were presented in the Great Hall. This was the time of the emergence of Rock and Roll. On one occasion, I obtained a copy of a song that had words that effectively or actually said 'I want to make love to you' – I think this was one of Elvis's hits of the day. The following morning I was summoned to the office of Dr Knight and told never to play such records that might encourage inappropriate thoughts in the School's pupils ever again.

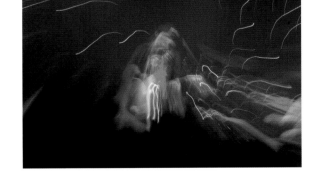

Peter Leach, St Anthony '63

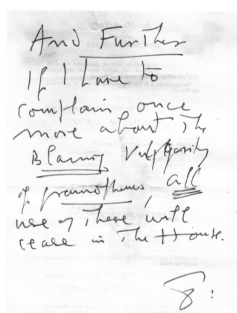

And Further
If I have to
complain once
more about the
Blaring Vulgarity
of gramophones, all
use of these will
cease in the House.

On one occasion during a whole school practice of 'The Messiah', Robin Miller pointed to me in the non-choir and said 'We'll do that again for Dickinson's benefit!' I never moved a finger out of place after that!

Peter Dickinson, Laundimer '59

I think, but am not certain, that the first broadcast performance of 'The Messiah' anywhere in the world was given by the School in 1922. It was performed by the whole School (including the non-choir) with an augmented school orchestra, and the visiting soloists included Carrie Tubb (whose son was then at Oundle), Dame Clara Butt, Ben Davis and Norman Alan. The transmitter was built by the Science department and the concert was heard as far afield as Copenhagen.

John Collcott, Laxton School '29

spring

'Going back to the spring term 1936, there was a period of torrential rain over several days which resulted in the River Nene overflowing its banks and creating huge lakes which attracted a wonderful array of wildfowl. The Headmaster, Kenneth Fisher, was a keen and well known ornithologist, and for several days he took groups of boys, members of the school Natural History Society, to watch those visitors, and no doubt instilled in many of them, including me, an abiding interest in 'bird watching''

(Bob Maslen-Jones, Ldr, '39)

Summer was a different story as Laxton Grammar School boarders were allowed to hire bicycles from Lane's in St Osyth's Lane or hire one of their skiffs, tied up under one of the arches of the North Bridge. In all seasons Laxton School boarders were allowed to walk and roam wherever they liked on Sunday afternoons as long as they were back in time for tea.

John Collcott, Laxton School '29

On Sundays Laxton Schoolboys formed up in the Cloisters, juniors wearing Eton collars and jackets, black striped trousers and straw hats and marched across the churchyard into the north transept of St Peter's Church to attend morning service and to listen to Canon Smalley Law.

John Collcott, Laxton School '29

I remember 'Jack-of-the-Forge' shoeing a horse; the acrid smell of burning hair; the horse, patient as Jack leant into its flank, his mouth bristling with slender curved nails with which he hammered the freshly tailored horse-shoe home....

Major Terence Tinsley, St Anthony '40

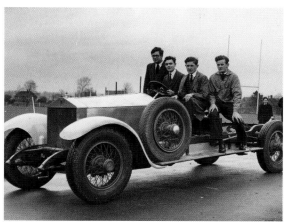

Only a few boys were needed to work in the Forge, which was often busy either shoeing working horses or repairing farm machinery because parts were always in short supply. Coke for the fires came from the gas works at the bottom of Blackpot Lane, just a short distance down the hill from the then Forge. This, and the warm foundry on casting days were always good places to be allocated in the winter terms.

Gordon Brooker, Laundimer '44

The instructor in the Foundry was easily angered. He used sometimes to throw small castings at mischievous boys. We put down a mould with no sand in the bottom half box. He poured on and on. No riser filled and suddenly a stream of liquid metal leaked out. Oh he was wild!

Geoffrey Bayley, St Anthony '47

When we were in the Metalshop we were made to line up at the beginning of the morning with our hands out, as if we were receiving communion bread, to be given a squirt of Rosalex hand protector from a grease gun.

Ian Sellars, Laxton '56

During a Biology class a boy in the back row was furtively trying to finish his 'prep' behind a pile of books. To get the boy's attention the teacher picked up the large pickled dogfish he was in the process of dissecting for our benefit and flung it at him. The slimy object hit the astonished lad fair and square on the forehead. We all cheered 'Good shot, sir!' and, attention restored, the class went on!

David Stembridge, Sanderson '56

'Bungy' Palmer, Senior Chemistry Master, small, round, short-sighted and cross-eyed. Ikey Hepburn, also a Chemistry Master but Deputy Headmaster, tall, genial, bespectacled. Coming from opposite directions round the corner of the Science Block, they collide violently. Peering angrily upwards Bungy exclaims 'Why don't you look where you're going?' Downwards came the reply 'Why don't you go where you're looking?'

Stewart Hamilton, Grafton '55 & many others!

In March 1938 I played the part of Dancy in the School Play. What the play was now escapes me. The female parts were played by masters' wives, but at one rehearsal none of them were able to come, and the producer Arthur Marshall proceeded to take all their places in turn, quickly reducing the whole cast to a state of helpless hysteria!

Richard Keynes, Laxton '38

The annual play in 1945 was Richard II in 'mediaeval' dress. Sir Stephen Scoop had holes in embarrassing places on his tights and the audience started to shout ribald comments more suitable to the Globe Theatre in the seventeenth century than the Great Hall. At the interval 'Gus' Stainforth mounted the stage and said 'I have never seen an audience of such uncultivated buffoons' and gave the whole School a dressing down which silenced the rowdy element for the duration.

Freddy Price, Laundimer '50

In respect of being beaten, I recall the piece of felt cut to fit the backside with elastic for waist and both legs. Very necessary if the house prefect was a Fives player. Very essential to make certain it was well knocked out before the event for a trace of dust at the first stroke gave the game away and you were forced to lower your trousers.

Richard Myott, School House '48

I recall the 'Boat Test' – in which new boys were thrown (fully clothed in thick rugger shirt, heavy cricket trousers, and rugger boots) into the River Nene near the bridge and boathouse – and required to swim 100 yds upstream (or was it downstream?). Somehow I managed to survive....

John Hadrill, Dryden '48

Coming back to the boathouse from an outing one cold, late afternoon, with 'Snappy' Priestman coxing, he looked over our shoulders at the Nene bridge and said: 'Oh look – two green elephants'. We considered him to be an eccentric, and were prepared for most things, but almost capsized at that one. But in fact, he was right. A circus had come to Oundle and two elephants, covered in tarpaulins to protect them from the cold, were indeed crossing the bridge. Dear 'Snappy'. We went on to win. 'They were good boys', he later said. 'They ignored everything I told them!'

Stewart Patrick, School House '56

111

The award of house or school colours in any sport was a matter for celebration by the whole house of the honoured boy. The celebration, normally at the house before lunch, involved de-bagging the new colour and throwing his trousers as high as possible into the trees outside.

Philip Bambury, School House '61

1967. I was in the US Army, patrolling the Vietnamese town of Bien Hoa. It was hot and dangerous, but I remembered marching for ten miles behind Colonel David Anderson at Oundle's CCF summer camp in Wales. Compared to that, Vietnam was a picnic.

Sir Howard Stringer, Laundimer '60

Sanderson House

25/8/51   Oundle

Northants

Dear Mum & Dad

I arrived back as you will see by this letter.
I went down to Mr Matthews on Saturday night and told him
about the gun. It may have made a little difference in his
opinion of me.

John Robinson, Sanderson '52

summer

'For clothing in the summer we wore a three piece grey flannel suit with a straw hat and black tie during the week, and in the winter a dark, almost black heavier suit with a cap and black tie. On Sundays throughout the year we wore black striped trousers with a black waistcoat and jacket and a black and white straw hat. In later years it became the practice to wear the grey flannel suit on weekdays all the year round, the younger boys wore starched Eton collars whilst the older boys wore white stiff collars. Black shoes and socks completed the dress.'

(Richard Metcalfe, New House, '39)

123

'The doctor will be looking at my leg today to see how it is. The Grafton boy didn't know he had kicked me, Dad, – I don't know who it was. But when you get flattened by three people, you can't tell what will happen.'

Colin Frizzell, Dryden '57
(From a letter home from the Sanatorium 1953)

In the summer, Laxton Grammar School boys, like Oundle boys, used to bathe in the River Nene, changing in a long wooden hut alongside the river. Boys were taught to dive in the deep water below the lock and were awarded 'blues' after swimming 100 yards, mostly entangled in weeds.

John Collcott, Laxton School '29

127

In the summer there was swimming weekly in the River Nene approached by a walk across fields and then through tall reeds infested with dragon flies. New boys started as 'mudlarks' wearing skimpy white trunks with pink stripes. After passing a test, dark blue trunks could be worn and access given to deeper water. The river was crystal clear with plenty of fish to be seen.

Richard Metcalfe, New House '39

131

When the Queen Mother came to open the new Cricket Pavilion for the Quatercentenary I ran like mad to get a position right in front of the balcony so that I could snap the occasion with my antique bellows camera. I was in the front row and right in the middle so I could take the perfect photograph. As soon as I could I rushed to the old museum in the Chapel Gardens to develop and print the masterpiece. When I had done so, and enlarged the image, I realised that an enormous microphone was right in front of the Queen Mother's face. All I can prove for posterity, therefore, is that the pavilion was opened by someone in a hat!

Beresford John Evitt, Laxton '58

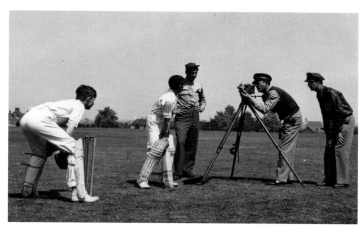

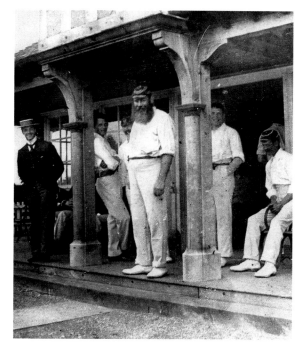

I recall being allowed to swim in the river in the summer term when the water rose above 60°F and being chucked into it in winter as a survival test to be a cox; endeavouring to construct a wireless, which I thought was very clever, and having it confiscated as they were not allowed in School House; seeing Clark Gable in USAAF uniform coming out of the paper shop opposite School House; and getting duffed up if I was served before those senior to me when queuing for a second helping!

Lancelot Foreman, School House '45

I well remember cycling with my pals to Polebrook and watching the 'Flying Fortress' bombers returning from their raids. On one occasion we were close to a crashed aircraft when Clark Gable arrived on the scene and in no uncertain language told us to 'hop it'.

Bob Devereux, Grafton '43

Sanderson House,
Oundle School,
Oundle,
Northants.

19/10/47

Dear Mum & Dad

Viscount Montgomery gave a very interesting lecture on the two battles of his North African Campaign, one was Alamein and the other was Mareth in Tunisia, he also told us how to beat Uppingham yesterday but the match never came off, he told us some confidential things about Stalin and the Russians, at the end he gave us the book about all his German Campaigns and asked the Head to give us a half holiday

John Robinson, Sanderson '52

During General Montgomery's visit to Oundle in 1948 I was delegated to meet his car on the Thrapston road to ensure his safe arrival. The car was impressive and I expressed my admiration. Monty carefully explained that it has two engines, which seemed rather improbable to an Oundelian. It was, of course, a V8 or 12. I often wondered who helped Monty over the technicalities of El Alamein.

Michael Bell, Laxton '48

29 June, 1927 Eclipse. We all got out of the train arranged by the School. Everyone was playing around with their masks. Suddenly the moon began to edge into the sun. We all watched with our masks, spellbound, and soon the sun began to disappear and darkness increased. The birds stopped singing and it wasn't long before the sun was obliterated except for a haze around the moon caused no doubt by illuminated atmosphere. Not long before the sun appeared and bit by bit daylight returned, the birds started singing again and we had a very short night no doubt. So back to the train and on to Oundle.

Denis Lacy-Hulbert, Bramston '28

I remember the occasion of the eclipse of the sun when we all travelled overnight with our sandwiches in the special train to some moor in Yorkshire. We stood waiting for the great occasion and were told that on no account should we look at the sun without the blue glass which had been given to each of us. At the critical moment a cloud came across the sun and I can recall the complete silence which descended on the world for the period of darkness.

Jack Barber, St Anthony '30

For farm work during the summer holidays we were paid sixpence (2.5 p) an hour. Of this two shillings (10 p) a day was meant to be deducted for our board and lodgings. Nice farmers, like the Berridges, never took the money and probably gave us more besides.

John Palmer, Bramston '46

Farming. During the summer holidays a lot of us went to local farms to help with the harvest. On the whole the farmers treated us very well. Myself and two others from Bramston went to Barnwell to the Berridge farm. (One of their sons who had been in Laundimer was killed in action after D Day). We were treated as one of the family, lived in a tent but fed with the family, and ate very well. To this day I can still remember some ham we had from one of their pigs which must have run into a tractor!

John Palmer, Bramston '46

Summer holidays in 1940s – helping local farmers. Driving Suffolk Punches towing haycarts. Great fun – volunteered to repeat following year, but harvest delayed so spent fortnight picking potatoes. Not such fun!

Lt Cdr Ken MacKenzie, Sanderson '42

143

During World War II we were invited to go to local farms during summer holidays to help with farm work for two weeks. Several Sidney boys went to a farm near Benefield. We were put to work pulling up wild oats each day – a back-breaking job for us – but our contribution to the war effort.

Gordon Oliver, Sidney '42

Wartime food was rationed, and boys are always hungry. In Laundimer we had access to sacks of onions and carrots in the cellar from the school farm which we boiled up on a primus in our study.

Ronny Price, Laundimer '43

During the War rationing was in force. We each had our own jam jar for sugar, and another for jam. There was about 6 ounces of sugar which lasted a week. The jam had to last a month. These were stored on shelves in the dining rooms. Sometimes Dudley Heesom did a deal with some local farmer and got extra fruit so that we got an extra issue of jam.

John Palmer, Bramston '46

A hot day on parade for the annual CCF inspection. The reviewing officer was late. At last a sports car roared to a halt behind us – a door slammed! 'Sorry I'm late' – Douglas Bader had arrived!

Sqn Ldr Tim Turnbull, Grafton '61

Group Captain Sir Douglas Bader was inspecting the annual CCF parade. The year? 1962? I was sporting a CND badge on my uniform. Approaching from my left he stumped down the row. He'd gone past me when he suddenly stopped and swung around, his left prosthetic leg swinging out, pre-empting John Cleese's TV efforts by several years.

'Boy,' he barked, pointing at my badge, 'do you believe in all that stuff?'

'Yes sir,' I replied.

'Good for you then,' he replied, swinging around and stumping off down the line.

Tony Handley, Laundimer '63

VE day. May 1945. There were no lessons that day. The Headmaster, Bud Fisher, was reputed to have said that this was the time when the Headmaster stayed in his study! Very wise, the pubs were full of boys drinking. Virtually the whole School took to the streets, and my abiding memory is of an American jeep with four very scared-looking soldiers in it trying to drive through to get away. Needless to say they were not harmed in any way and made their escape eventually.

John Palmer, Bramston '46

I recall my Father taking my brother and myself for an interview with Dr Fisher. My Father asked for a copy of the school rules, Bud looked up sharply and said quietly, 'We have no school rules. We rely on common sense.'

Richard Metcalfe, New House '39

'The 'Peter Scott' statue has suffered further indignities to its prominent parts, last week with rain from its upheld umbrella, this week from the bursar's staff frantically sandpapering off the patriotic red, white and blue paint.'

Rod Alexander, School House '61

(From a letter home)

oundle – a school for all seasons

'For the school debate 'Boggy' (Mr Cartwright) wore a double-breasted pinstripe jacket, tartan shirt, khaki shorts and Wellingtons. His face was horribly swollen by a bee sting.'

David Hancock, Dryden '57
(Extract from diary, 21 July 1956)

Whilst battling to obtain an Oxford and Cambridge entrance pass in my final term I was notified by my housemaster, B.K. Harris, to 'pack my bags' as, on the final day of the exams I would be escorted to Oundle station and put on a train home. This, apparently, was for my own good as it was thought that I would attempt to climb the church spire – or carry out some equally unlikely feat. (Shame on you, 'Beaky'!)

Tony Briggs, School House '49

'We must on no account panic. But I do think that the time has come for a certain amount of controlled urgency.'

David Hancock, Dryden '57
(Rolf Barber to Mod. VIC shortly before A-level German exam, summer 1955)

I used to look after orphaned birds in a cage I built behind Old Chapel. The most spectacular was a heron. On Speech Day, it gave a magnificent display of its fish-catching skills – standing in a hip-bath on the front lawn of Laxton. It also used to ride around perched on the handlebars of my bicycle.

Clive Minton, Laxton '53

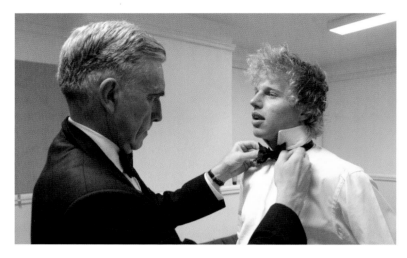

*A lady dancing teacher from Peterborough used
to teach ballroom dancing in the Long Room
some Saturday evenings in the Christmas term –
waltz, foxtrot, quick step, tango, gallop and the
Charleston. After stacking up all the desks to one
side and polishing the floor the boys changed
into cricket flannels and blazers – great fun!*

John Collcott, Laxton School '29

'You boys are using far too many toilet rolls. Three pieces should be enough, if not, turn them over and use the other side.'

Jack Barber, St Anthony '30
(H.M. 'John' King, New House notices after breakfast)

'The human digestive system is like the fire in a boiler. If it gets clogged up RAKE IT OUT.'

Richard Haigh, New House '41
(John King's last address to boys of New House on his retirement c.1940)

'The invention of the water closet in the sixteenth century struck the death knell of English agriculture.'

Hugh Playfair, Bramston '54
(A reminiscence of German lessons by Bill Cartwright)

O.O. WEEK-END.

It was a silent Autumn morn——
Most glorious of days;
The birds were singing in the trees,
The sun shed golden rays.

But soon the peace in a thousand parts
Was shattered beyond repair,
For round the corner slick and proud
And shining in the air,
There came the first of the many cars
Which Old Oundelians bear.

His hair was long, his clothes were loud,
His O.O. scarf flew free.
His bearing made clear to all those near
That he (take note) was HE:

"I am an Old Oundelian,
I have a small, fast car,
I drink nine pints of beer a day
And smoke ten fags an hour.
And all you chaps, who are still at school——
I don't know who you are!"

He pulled his cap down over his eyes.
Nimbly he started the car.
A roar, some fumes, and he was lost——
Again we could breathe pure air.